More Than Multisite

Inside Today's Methods and Models for Launching New Congregations

A Barna Report Produced in Partnership
with Cornerstone Knowledge Network

Contents

Introduction

When Scripture introduces the Church in Acts 2, it paints a picture of a people fervently committed to their faith. They devoted themselves to Christian teachings, gathered regularly, shared meals, built community and served the poor. They also grew—quickly. "And the Lord added to their number daily those who were being saved," according to Acts 2:47.

The definitions, goals and metrics of church growth have evolved in the centuries since. Today, there are entire networks of proliferating churches, with their own structures and terminologies.

Many credit the now-common concept of "multisite churches"—churches with multiple locations—to large megachurches that had grown rapidly and needed to scale up quickly to accommodate that growth. Early pioneers of this approach include North Coast Church in Vista, California; Seacoast Church in South and North Carolina; Community Christian Church in Naperville, Illinois; and New Life Chicago.

Since these forerunners popularized the idea of multiple sites in the '90s, smaller churches have also begun to try their hand at expanding. Additionally, today's models of launching and growing churches can take a plethora of forms: multiple campuses with a broadcast sermon, individual churches under an umbrella brand, parish model church plants and more.

Barna Group and Cornerstone Knowledge Network (on behalf of Aspen Group and Fishhook) undertook this research to learn more about the current culture and methods of planting and growing congregations. Our teams wanted to know: How do pastors translate a sense of mission to a new context? How does expansion affect decision making about church facilities, finances and staff? How does a reproducing ministry define success—and failure? What are the risks, roadblocks and red flags of attempting significant growth?

As a first step, the Barna team conducted 31 in-depth interviews with leaders of multisite and planting churches, including some consultants who have worked with numerous such churches over the years.

Then, a survey was conducted with a similar audience. In order to achieve a representative sample of multisite and planting churches, participants were invited from national lists of senior pastors and screened for inclusion based on:

1. The type of church(es) they work with (multisite, planting or co-located congregations, defined in more detail in chapter 1 and in the Methodology in the Appendix)
2. Their role (those with sufficient involvement in decision making to give insight into the strategies and operations of these churches)

After cleaning and screening out data from any churches that didn't have an *active* multisite or church planting ministry, our respondent set included 222 church leaders, distributed as follows:

- 90 percent senior pastors
- 5 percent executive pastors / directors / chief operating officers
- 5 percent campus or assistant pastors
- 56 percent oversee one church; 44 percent oversee multiple churches

Our teams went into this study thinking that leaders in growing churches want to know how to plant or "go multisite" and to learn best practices in terms of branding, facilities, organizational structures, and so on. In the process, we found two important tenets of effective growth models:

- Nearly every reproducing church is *primarily* motivated by a desire to live out a specific *calling* to reach a community (whether a neighborhood or a region) with the gospel

- *Leadership* is one of the key determinants of the pace and model of growth

This was encouraging news: that Jesus' Great Commission ("Therefore, go and make disciples of all the nations, baptizing them in the name of the Father and the Son and the Holy Spirit," Matt. 28:19) and his call to church leaders ("He said to his disciples, 'The harvest is great, but the workers are few,'" Matt. 9:37) are the key underpinnings of the present advance of church plants and multisite campuses.

In sharing this data, our hope is that churches considering whether to launch new congregations, or already preparing for such a transition, can minimize challenges or regrets and improve the effectiveness of their ministry. On whatever scale it occurs, healthy church expansion requires strategy—not merely for the growth of a congregation or the construction of a building, but ultimately for the spread of the gospel.

Church expansion requires strategy—not merely for the growth of a congregation or the construction of a building, but ultimately for the spread of the gospel

1 Models for Growth

In an effort to better understand the ways in which churches reproduce, researchers wanted to identify different models of growth. These models could provide helpful insight to and explanation of some of the choices churches make when it comes to identity, leadership, operations and more.

It was a challenge in itself, however, for researchers first to identify true "models," because every church or campus has its own unique story. Here are just some of the extreme variables in the findings:

- One out of four churches are over 100 years old when they launch their first multisite campus or church plant
- Twenty-nine percent have been part of a merger with, or acquisition of, another church
- The total number of adult attendees across churches / campuses ranges from 18 to 25,000

Having looked at the data from these churches in a variety of ways, the clearest distinctions emerged when researchers separate them by *the number of locations* and whether they consider these churches to be *multisite* (campuses that are part of a single church) or *church plants* (separate churches intended to operate independently at some point). There seem to be natural divisions between churches that have two or three locations versus four or more, and between those who adopt a multisite, planting or co-location strategy.

Among those with up to three locations, there are a variety of unique situations. Some are novices in the multisite or church-planting worlds, but have every intention of continuing to add to their ministry. Others tried it and either do not wish to repeat the experience (sometimes because of the challenges they faced), or have fulfilled their objective(s) and do not have plans to continue. These churches are dubbed "Beginners" since they are either new to the model or have only tried it once or twice.

Among those with four or more locations, there seems to be an intentional strategy of continuing to plant or add sites—an informed perspective based on past experiences with accelerated church growth. Accordingly, these churches are "Strategists."

In this report, the findings are analyzed using the following five categories[*]:

1. **Multisite Beginners:** a single church with two or three total locations or campuses

2. **Planting Beginners:** two or three semi-independent churches, where the "daughter" churches are considered church plants

3. **Multisite Strategists:** a single church with four or more total locations or campuses

4. **Planting Strategists:** four or more semi-independent churches, where the "daughter" churches are considered church plants

5. **Location Partners:** a separate congregation meeting at, and sharing resources with, another church (for example, a ministry reaching a specific demographic group, such as a young adult congregation or an international group with services in a different language)

---

[*] A note from the researchers: By dividing our sample into multiple groups, the size of each group is relatively small: approximately 40 pastors per group. However, the data show more statistically significant differences when dividing the church types in this way, due to the variation in responses between a multisite or church plant and between a larger network and a smaller one.

Distribution Within this Study

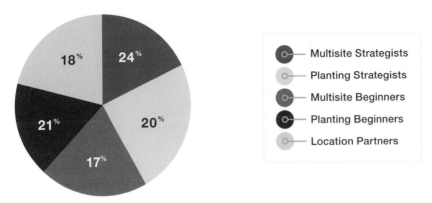

- **Multisite Strategists** — 24%
- **Planting Strategists** — 20%
- **Multisite Beginners** — 17%
- **Planting Beginners** — 21%
- **Location Partners** — 18%

Total Number of Church Locations: Strategists

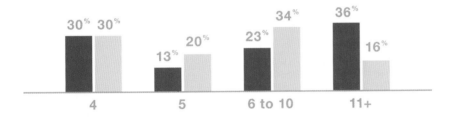

	4	5	6 to 10	11+
Multisite Strategists	30%	13%	23%	36%
Planting Strategists	30%	20%	34%	16%

Beginners & Location Partners

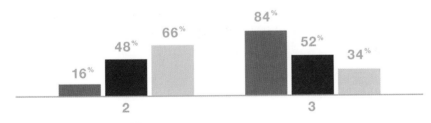

	2	3
Multisite Beginners	16%	84%
Planting Beginners	48%	52%
Location Partners	66%	34%

March 7–April 6, 2016, N=222.

Attendance

According to their number of locations, those with a multisite or church planting model also have the greatest number of attendees across all campuses and services: a median of 550 for multisite and 625 for church plants. The range varies significantly here, with 8 percent of church plants and 12 percent of multisite churches having 5,000 or more, up to 25,000.

Multisite Beginners have more attendees on average (median 355) than Planting Beginners (median 263), which suggests that size factors into their decision to opt for a multisite model. Indeed, 44 percent of Multisite Beginners have 500 or more in attendance across campuses. Congregations that are Location Partners have the smallest number of total attendees, indicating that their separate congregations may be smaller in size; co-locating is less a growth strategy than a way of reaching a special-interest group.

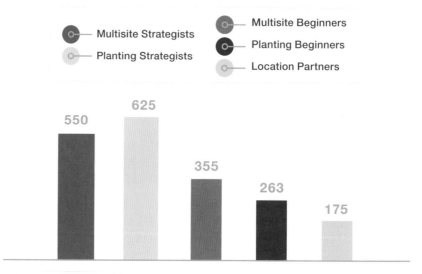

Median Number of Adult Attendees Across All Campuses & Services

- Multisite Strategists
- Planting Strategists
- Multisite Beginners
- Planting Beginners
- Location Partners

550 | 625 | 355 | 263 | 175

March 7–April 6, 2016, *N*=222.

Timing

Typically when churches start to contemplate a strategic growth model, they are already well established.

Churches that pursue a multisite model tend to be older than those that plant. A church may experience a rotation of pastors or an evolution of their congregation over time. At some point they reach a critical mass and feel called to add a new campus. For the average multisite church (Strategists and Beginners combined), this occurs at 38 years. Only one out of 10 attempts multisite within the first five years—but at the other end of the spectrum, one-third of Multisite Beginners launch their first daughter campus at *100 years* or older!

Planting Strategists have the youngest median age (14 years), suggesting they have a clear strategy to multiply even when they start their original church. One-third of this group plants its first daughter church within the *first five years* of its lifecycle. By contrast, only one out of five Planting Beginners start planting within five years. The median age at which they first plant is 20 years.

Typically when churches start to contemplate a strategic growth model, they are already well established

Median Age of Sending / Original Church When Growth Strategy Launched

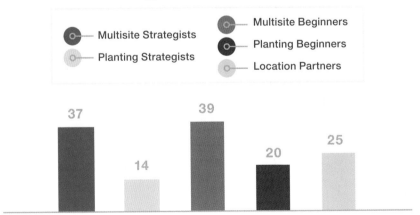

March 7–April 6, 2016, *N*=222.

An exception to the pattern of expansion after becoming established is among Location Partners, 17 percent of which start when the original church starts. However, many of these also co-locate later in their lifecycle, with a median age of 25 years when the congregation begins its sharing model.

Financial Stability

About half of churches become financially self-sufficient by around the two-year mark. There is no clear correlation between type of church (multisite or church plant) and the length of time it takes to become self-sustaining.

Time Until Campus Reaches Financial Self-Sufficiency

More than 5 years
3–5 years
1–2 years
Less than 1 year
Not self-sustaining yet

March 7–April 6, 2016, *N*=222.

Yet there seems to be an understanding among some parent churches or planting networks that certain campuses may never reach self-sufficiency, such as those in inner city neighborhoods or that minister to people in economically strained areas. In these cases the whole network of churches is able to carry the cost, making a church in such a neighborhood financially feasible, when it might not have been under other conditions. It is these churches' way of loving their city.

Expectations

How does the reality of launching a new congregation compare with the expectations ministry leaders had before they began? Do churches want to repeat the process? Few report it is easier than they anticipated. About one-third of leaders say it is harder than they expected.

Those with a multisite strategy are most likely to feel the pain of expansion. This is because, as they expand into a network of five, six or more locations, the effort to coordinate and maintain consistency across campuses grows exponentially. At this point, some multisite churches evolve into a combination strategy of multiplication: spinning off some campuses or planting new semi-independent churches out of either the main church or daughter campuses. (There may be a variety of drivers behind these different approaches, which we will explore later in this report, but the main idea is that complexity increases when churches exceed four locations.)

About one-third of leaders say launching a new congregation is harder than they expected

Reality vs. Expectations of Launching a New Congregation

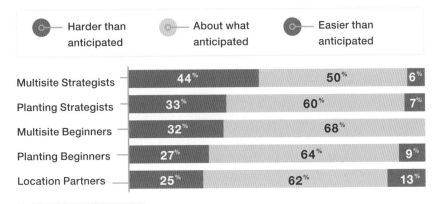

March 7–April 6, 2016, *N*=222.

Despite their challenges, most churches—whether multisite or planting—intend to continue with their strategy. Planting Strategists are most committed to their model, and larger churches (with 500 or more attendees across all locations) are more likely to continue than smaller churches. Location Partners are the only group in which a significant proportion are either unsure (39%) or unlikely (22%) to co-locate again—further substantiating the idea that these congregations are a method for serving a specific group, rather than a growth strategy for the ministry overall.

Do You Intend to Continue with Your Growth Strategy?

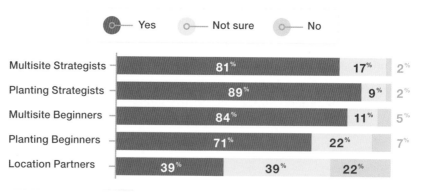

March 7–April 6, 2016, N=222.

Nearly half of churches (48%) are unsure when they will open a new location, but those that do have a timeline anticipate two years or less until their next expansion. This is fairly consistent across models. The relatively short timeline, and the commitment to maintain growth, suggest great enthusiasm for their model and conviction about their calling.

More Than Multisite

When Churches Plan to Launch Their Next Campus or Plant

% among churches with a timeline to expand

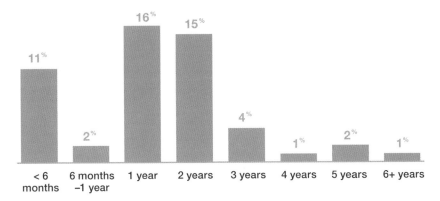

< 6 months	6 months –1 year	1 year	2 years	3 years	4 years	5 years	6+ years
11%	2%	16%	15%	4%	1%	2%	1%

March 7–April 6, 2016, *n*=94.

When Expansion Stops

Sometimes a church must close a campus. In other cases, they start a spinoff campus or church. One out of five churches has experienced a closing or cutting of ties with a campus (79% have done neither).

One out of five churches has closed or cut ties with a campus

Closed a Campus

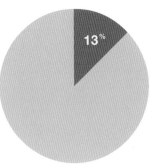

13%

Cut Ties with a Campus

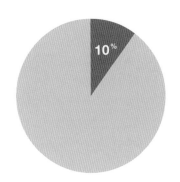

10%

March 7–April 6, 2016, *N*=222.

Low attendance is by far the most common reason for closing a campus, with 82 percent of those who have done so citing this reason. But other common challenges include leadership issues or turnover (32%) or financial problems (29% say the campus is expensive to maintain, 21% cite insufficient giving).

One pastor recalls closing a campus that started out somewhat unhealthy: "We planted a campus in a town that was made up of people who were leaving other churches because of issues they had. They were disgruntled; it wasn't the best foundation to build on. It didn't work. We closed that campus. We didn't count the cost early on, just got excited about starting campuses."

Why Close a Campus?

% among churches that have closed a campus

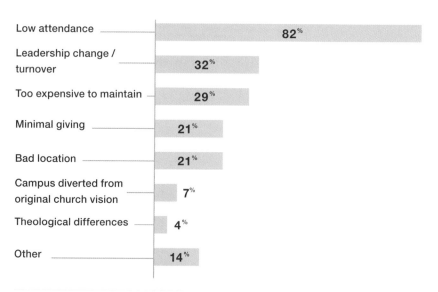

Low attendance — 82%
Leadership change / turnover — 32%
Too expensive to maintain — 29%
Minimal giving — 21%
Bad location — 21%
Campus diverted from original church vision — 7%
Theological differences — 4%
Other — 14%

March 7–April 6, 2016, *n*=28 (small base).

When a church cuts ties with a campus, one common challenge is a campus' vision diverting from that of the sending church (35%). However, a separation is most likely to occur due to success: 48 percent part ways after becoming self-sustaining and autonomous.

Brian Bloye of West Ridge Church in Dallas, Georgia, describes this encouraging transition: "As time goes on, as we're seeing that they're growing in leadership and able to handle themselves financially, we start loosening the reins a little bit. It's kind of like raising a child, to be honest with you. As we're sending them out, we give them more and more rope."

Why Cut Ties with a Campus?

% among churches who cut ties with a campus

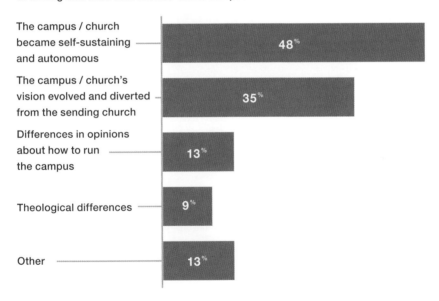

March 7–April 6, 2016, *n*=23 (small base).

Perhaps just as important as the ultimate success or failure of a new church or campus is the motivation behind starting one in the first place. In the next chapter, we look at the impetus guiding each church's expansion model.

Mergers & Acquisitions

A subcategory of strategies for adding church locations is the process of merging or acquiring another church. Approximately three out of 10 churches in this study (29%) have experienced a merger or acquisition. Most often this is a single event (64%), though about one-

Immanuel Baptist Church in Lexington, Kentucky. "There is still life in an old church, and we can rebirth that vision and energy again."

Other mergers have more to do with fit or chemistry between the existing churches. Forty-seven percent of

Experienced a Merger or Acquisition

If So, How Many?

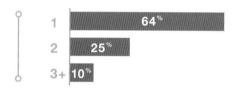

March 7–April 6, 2016, *N*=222.

third (35%) have been a part of two or more mergers or acquisitions. These churches are equally likely to be multisite or church plants, but merger and acquisition activity is more common among larger churches.

Leaders cite a variety of motivations for merging with or acquiring another church. Location (56%), immediate availability of a church (52%) and a suitable facility (50%)—all practical considerations—are most common.

According to one pastor who participated in the depth interviews, in an area where many older, traditional churches have experienced a significant decline in attendance, it is becoming commonplace for these older churches to approach newer, larger or more contemporary ministries and ask to be acquired, in an effort to bring new life to their facility and congregation. This solves a challenge for expanding multisite churches by providing a suitable, readily available space to meet, perhaps in an underserved location, while also restoring the church—in essence, a "win-win" for everyone.

"My heart beats for established churches who have seen better days," says Ron Edmondson, senior pastor of

churches that merged had an existing relationship with a church, and a similar number cited the compatibility of the churches (41%).

Zac Allen, founding pastor of Fellowship Bible Church in Austin, Texas, shares an example of how such a merger can also solve an operational challenge for a church plant: "Most assume a church merger involves a healthy church saving a dying congregation. In our case, it began with our elders considering the unique challenges of having almost a 2-to-1 adult-child ratio at our Sunday worship service, and realizing future growth would likely reflect that same dynamic."

Allen says the ministry had an existing relationship with Austin Stone, a local multisite church, and agreed to merge due to the compatibility of the congregations, church culture and location. The merger was a successful grafting of two churches and also provided much-needed resources for the plant to continue to grow—especially in their children's programs.

"The merger was the hardest and best thing we went through as a church and personally as a leader," Allen continues. "In the end, 87 percent of our members

Why Was Merger / Acquisition a Good Fit?

% among churches that have merged or acquired

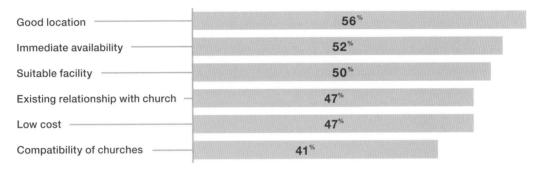

- Good location — 56%
- Immediate availability — 52%
- Suitable facility — 50%
- Existing relationship with church — 47%
- Low cost — 47%
- Compatibility of churches — 41%

March 7–April 6, 2016, *n*=64 U.S. pastors who have experienced a merger or acquisition.

stayed through the transition, and ultimately learned that this wasn't our church all along; Austin Bible belonged to Jesus."

Most churches that have undergone a merger or acquisition say their experience was positive overall, yet their commentary reveals some challenges. For example, multisite churches are more likely to say the experience was positive because they gained a new facility without taking on much financial burden. However, church plants more often say the new facility created new financial strain.

Several pastors express the difficulty of taking on "dying churches." Such ministries may bring with them years of baggage and, too often, disgruntled members. Many church leaders explain that the unity (or lack thereof) of the two groups involved in the merger plays a significant role in its success.

Result of Merger / Acquisition

% among churches that have merged or acquired

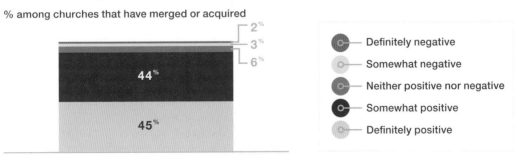

- 2%
- 3%
- 6%
- 44%
- 45%

○— Definitely negative
○— Somewhat negative
○— Neither positive nor negative
○— Somewhat positive
○— Definitely positive

March 7–April 6, 2016, *n*=64 U.S. pastors who have experienced a merger or acquisition.

Strength in Numbers

Exploring the 5 major models of church expansion

Adding a church location can be a complicated process, unique to the geography, size, vision and finances of the ministry. But our research reveals a few key models for doing so, based on strategy and number of locations. One important thing they have in common: A majority from each group intend to continue with their chosen method of church expansion. Here's an introduction to the faces and spaces of these movements, as well as their core motivations.

Multisite Beginner

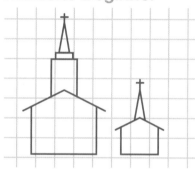

A single church with two or three total locations or campuses

Make up 17 percent of the pastors surveyed

 A median of 355 attendees across all campuses and services

Most have 3 locations (84%)

Usually employ 2-3 full-time pastors and 1-2 part-time pastors*

Typically, the original church is 39 years old when it goes multisite

Why? "To be more effective in reaching a city or region" (37%)

Planting Beginner

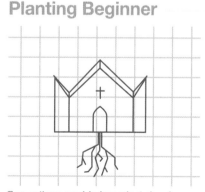

Two or three semi-independent churches, where the daughter churches are considered church plants

Make up 21 percent of the pastors surveyed

 A median of 263 attendees across all campuses and services

 Most have 3 locations (52%)

 Usually employ 2-3 full-time pastors and 1.5 part-time pastors*

 Typically, the sending church is 20 years old when it begins planting

 Why? "To be more effective in reaching a city or region" (41%)

Multisite Strategist

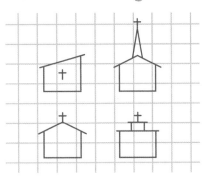

A single church organization with four or more total locations or campuses

 Make up 24 percent of the pastors surveyed

 A median of 550 attendees across all campuses and services

 Most have 11+ locations (36%) or 4 locations (30%)

 Usually employ 2-5 full-time pastors and 2-3 part-time pastors*

 Typically, the original church is 37 years old when it goes multisite

Why? "To be more effective in reaching a city or region" (43%)

Planting Strategist

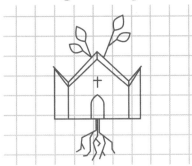

Four or more semi-independent churches, where the "daughter" churches are considered church plants

 Make up 20 percent of the pastors surveyed

 A median of 625 attendees across all campuses and services

 Most have 6–10 locations (34%) or 4 locations (30%)

 Usually employ 3-6 full-time pastors and 3-5 part-time pastors*

 Typically, the sending church is 14 years old when it begins planting

Why? "To fulfill a mission or strategic plan" (45%)

Location Partner

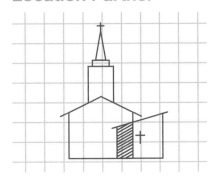

A separate congregation meeting at, and sharing resources with, another church

 Make up 18 percent of the pastors surveyed

 A median of 175 attendees across all campuses and services

 Most have 2 locations (66%)

 Usually employ 1-2 full-time pastors and 1 or no part-time pastor*

 Typically, the original church is 25 years old when it co-locates

Why? "To be more effective in reaching a city or region" (41%)

*Per site

2 Ministry Strategies

What drives or motivates churches to pursue various expansion strategies? *Geographical outreach, mission* and *calling* are the top three primary reasons cited by most churches. Researchers had concluded from the in-depth interviews that need for space or an existing plan for growth were the main drivers of expansion, and so were surprised and encouraged that more missional motivations emerged from the data findings.

In fact, facility constraints or accommodating growth barely register as primary reasons (just 2% among Planting Beginners). Even among the secondary reasons for adopting their particular model, these drivers are mentioned by only one-quarter or less of any group.

There are some subtle differences between the groups that align with their expansion strategies. For example, Multisite Strategists (43%) are significantly more focused than Planting Strategists (23%) on geographical reach. They are also most likely to say tailoring to different demographics is an important secondary goal (38%).

Additionally, space-related factors come into play as a secondary reason significantly more for multisite churches than for others.

Planting Strategists are so named because they have a clear church-planting strategy, and 45 percent of these churches saying their primary reason for planting is their mission / strategic plan (compared with 19% of Multisite Strategists and 21% of Multisite Beginners). They are also more likely than other groups to cite leadership growth as a motivation for planting, though only 16 percent say this is a secondary reason.

These findings reflect what researchers heard from in-depth interviews with leaders in multisite and church planting networks.

45% of Planting Strategists say their primary reason for planting is to fulfill their mission or strategic plan

Primary Reason to Pursue Growth Strategy

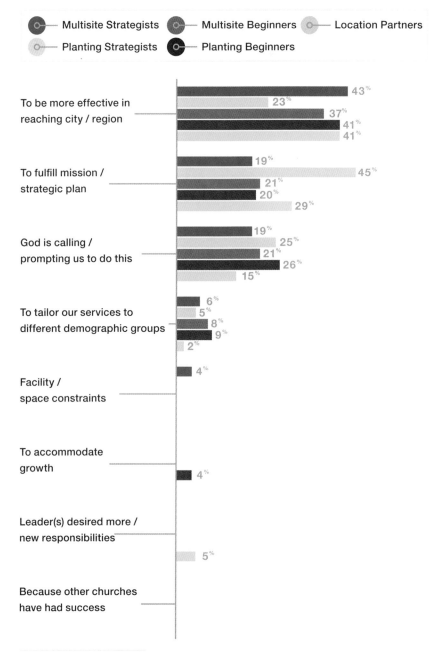

- ●—— Multisite Strategists ◐—— Multisite Beginners ○—— Location Partners
- ◔—— Planting Strategists ●—— Planting Beginners

To be more effective in reaching city / region
- 43%
- 23%
- 37%
- 41%
- 41%

To fulfill mission / strategic plan
- 19%
- 45%
- 21%
- 20%
- 29%

God is calling / prompting us to do this
- 19%
- 25%
- 21%
- 26%
- 15%

To tailor our services to different demographic groups
- 6%
- 5%
- 8%
- 9%
- 2%

Facility / space constraints
- 4%

To accommodate growth
- 4%

Leader(s) desired more / new responsibilities
- 5%

Because other churches have had success

March 7–April 6, 2016, *N*=222.

Secondary Reasons to Pursue Growth Strategy

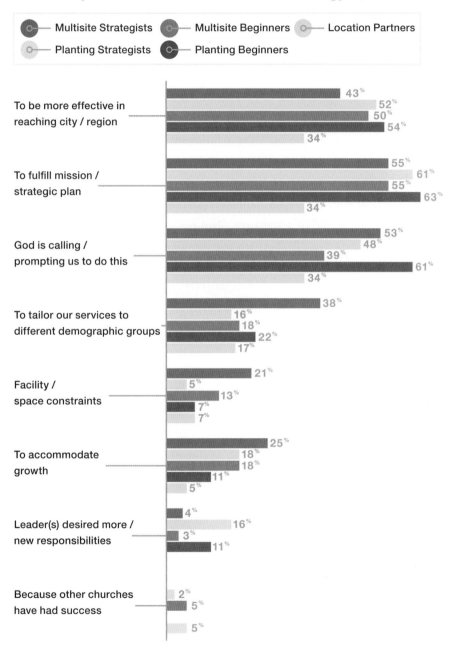

Legend:
- Multisite Strategists
- Multisite Beginners
- Location Partners
- Planting Strategists
- Planting Beginners

To be more effective in reaching city / region
- 43%
- 52%
- 50%
- 54%
- 34%

To fulfill mission / strategic plan
- 55%
- 61%
- 55%
- 63%
- 34%

God is calling / prompting us to do this
- 53%
- 48%
- 39%
- 61%
- 34%

To tailor our services to different demographic groups
- 38%
- 16%
- 18%
- 22%
- 17%

Facility / space constraints
- 21%
- 5%
- 13%
- 7%
- 7%

To accommodate growth
- 25%
- 18%
- 18%
- 11%
- 5%

Leader(s) desired more / new responsibilities
- 4%
- 16%
- 3%
- 11%

Because other churches have had success
- 2%
- 5%
- 5%

March 7–April 6, 2016, *N*=222.

"Space [was a factor], in that every time we launched a campus and drew people out of [our largest campus], it would refill. It never had a ton of empty space," says Bill Steele, director of operations for McLean Bible Church, which has multiple campuses in the Washington, D.C., area. "But also, vision [drove us], because ultimately the goal is to bring souls into the kingdom. We're not interested in getting bigger to say we're bigger. Rank is irrelevant. So if we saw an opportunity open up to create a campus—like a building opening up in an area we'd been praying about—we took it. We saw it as a sign from the Lord."

Jen Wilson, pastor of Wheatland Salem Church in Naperville and Oswego, Illinois, employs a common metaphor for the multisite approach: "sharing the DNA" of a ministry. "Not because Wheatland was too full; it wasn't," she says. "Rather, we felt the DNA of this particular United Methodist Church could influence this other community in a positive way."

Paul Gotthardt pastors Life Baptist Church, which has two campuses in Las Vegas, Nevada. "Our plan from the beginning was to start a church that would start churches," he acknowledges. "We never wanted to have 50 acres of land with a massive building where everyone can be on one campus. But we did want a strong base where a church could grow up to a healthy 1,500 to 2,000 [attendees] and continue to send 200 to 300 out to start other churches."

3 Culture

Although churches that have adopted similar growth strategies share some core motivations, individual ministries vary in their style, tone, ethos and local presence. When launching a new campus or location, every decision contributes, intentionally or unintentionally, to a church's unique culture.

In this chapter we examine the nuances of establishing new congregations: the ways churches market themselves, how launch teams distribute responsibility, what leaders expect from expansion—and, ultimately, how the goal of reproduction impacts the culture of a church and the community it inhabits.

Identity & Branding

One feature that often distinguishes a multisite from a church plant is its name or identity. More often than not, multisite churches maintain a strong brand affiliation with a mother church, while church plants tend to be more independent. However, researchers found this is not a universal truth; as these growth models evolve, so do their branding and communications efforts.

Multisite Strategist (65%) and Multisite Beginner (58%) churches are much more likely to keep the same name or identity as the sending church—almost three times as likely as Planting Strategists (23%) and Planting Beginners (10%). Conversely, Planting Strategists, Planting Beginners and Location Partners tend to adopt their own identity, since these congregations often begin as separate entities.

Whatever their choice, churches feel good about their approach, whether they develop an individual identity or keep the same name as the sending church. In either case, most believe the benefits outweigh the challenges.

Expansion Brand Strategy

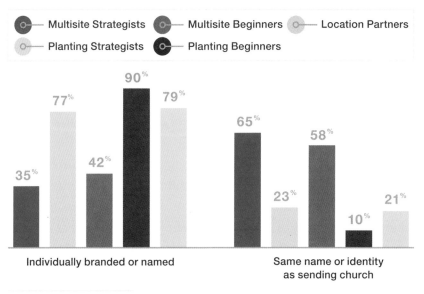

Legend:
— Multisite Strategists — Multisite Beginners — Location Partners
— Planting Strategists — Planting Beginners

Individually branded or named
- 35%
- 77%
- 42%
- 90%
- 79%

Same name or identity as sending church
- 65%
- 23%
- 58%
- 10%
- 21%

March 7–April 6, 2016, *N*=222.

Among campuses that share branding, 54% believe name recognition attracts new visitors

The greatest benefit of developing individual branding, according to those who adopted this strategy, is giving leaders more ownership of their church or campus (72%), along with reflecting the local context (58%). For churches that share central branding, on the other hand, alignment (72%) and efficiencies (70%) are most important; about half believe name recognition of the sending church attracts new visitors (54%).

The sending church's brand recognition may influence where and how a new campus is established in the first place. Layne Schranz says this is a driving factor for Church of the Highlands, the Birmingham, Alabama, church where he is associate pastor. "Where the Church of the Highlands (COH) brand is known and recognized, we open a campus. [This is the] best way to steward our influence, reach people and engage more people with less cost more quickly and successfully. But where the COH brand is not known, we usually help plant a church."

When it comes to communications in general, churches often underestimate the amount of time and work that goes into producing

Effects of Individual Branding

% among those who opted for separate branding

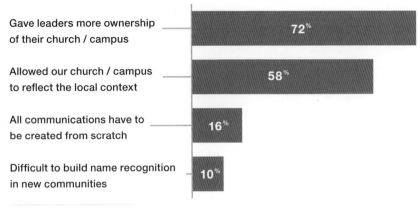

Gave leaders more ownership of their church / campus — 72%

Allowed our church / campus to reflect the local context — 58%

All communications have to be created from scratch — 16%

Difficult to build name recognition in new communities — 10%

March 7–April 6, 2016, *N*=126.

Effects of Same Branding

% among those who opted for centralized branding

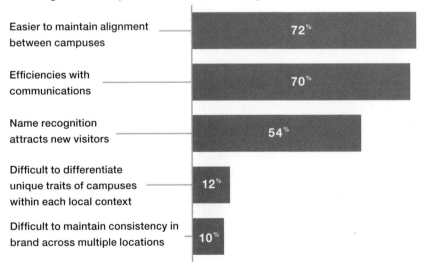

Easier to maintain alignment between campuses — 72%

Efficiencies with communications — 70%

Name recognition attracts new visitors — 54%

Difficult to differentiate unique traits of campuses within each local context — 12%

Difficult to maintain consistency in brand across multiple locations — 10%

March 7–April 6, 2016, *N*=69.

clear, compelling marketing and announcements, from websites and flyers to worship service visuals. Compared to multisite churches, few church plants enjoy centralized or shared responsibility for communications. Multisites, on the other hand, are more likely to leverage communications as a way of maintaining a consistent brand or identity. Nearly all have at least shared responsibility for communications, and one-third of Multisite Strategists (36%) and half of Multisite Beginners (50%) use completely centralized communication. This is a larger percentage than those who report a single brand identity with the same name as their sending church, which suggests that consistent branding extends beyond name to include the look and feel of a variety of public-facing communications. Additionally, these multisite churches may be tapping into useful resources at the central church where secondary campus resources may not yet exist.

Jim Tomberlin, founder and CEO of MultiSite Solutions, offers some prompts for churches trying to determine an appropriate strategy for the marketing and communications for a new location: "Live in the tension of consistency on one end and contextualization on the other. What needs to be identical and what just needs to be identifiable? What needs to be standardized with our best practices, and what needs to be organic locally?"

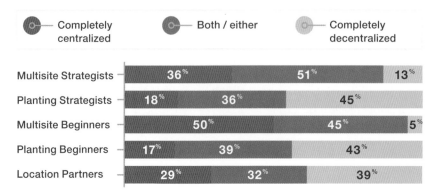

Communications: Centralized or Decentralized?

◐— Completely centralized   ◐— Both / either   ◐— Completely decentralized

	Completely centralized	Both / either	Completely decentralized
Multisite Strategists	36%	51%	13%
Planting Strategists	18%	36%	45%
Multisite Beginners	50%	45%	5%
Planting Beginners	17%	39%	43%
Location Partners	29%	32%	39%

March 7–April 6, 2016, N=222.

Positive & Negative Impacts

The upsides and the downsides of expansion shape the culture of both the sending church and the new church or campus. Multisite and church planting leaders interviewed by Barna reveal a range of results stemming from their growth strategies—positive, negative and unexpected. Although some in-depth interviewees relayed stories of fatigued volunteers, financial strains or operational glitches in the early years, the survey data present a more balanced picture.*

When discussing the top positive results of opening a new church or campus, more than half of pastors say it benefited the surrounding community. Mark DeYmaz experienced this when Mosaic, the Central Arkansas church where he is directional leader, took over an abandoned space: "We cleaned it up and affected the community. It was next to a shopping center; there was a crime reduction throughout the area," DeYmaz recalls. "We are not just trying to see souls saved. We want to bring redemption to an entire community, specifically our zip code. I think that's more fruitful, ultimately, than more people in my pews."

An additional one-third of pastors says the new church revitalized the congregation itself, an effect also mirrored in Barna's in-depth conversations with leaders. Many leaders talk about the phenomenon of members growing disengaged or disconnected in larger churches. Yet, when these same members are activated to launch a new campus or church, they often feel a new sense of ownership and mission that serves to develop lay leadership and revitalizes the congregation as a whole.

More than half also point to positive benefits for leadership development, something of particular relevance to Planting Strategy churches, which tend to plant based on their pipeline of church leaders. Tom Hughes, co-lead pastor at Los Angeles' Christian Assembly, offers

> When members are activated to launch a new campus or church, they often feel a new sense of ownership and mission

---

* A note from the researchers: We often find that respondents in quantitative surveys report a slightly more positive assessment of their situation, compared with qualitative interviews, in which respondents relay personal stories and experiences with deeper emotion.

an example of how expansion can be a turning point for leadership: "The moment we went to two sides of the street, we added more pastoral staff, so that created the opportunity to raise up additional leaders," Hughes says. "Having two venues running simultaneously forced us to be better at lay leadership development and staff leadership development."

Three-quarters of church plant leaders, compared with just over half of multisite leaders, mention that launching a new location provided more opportunities for lay leader development.

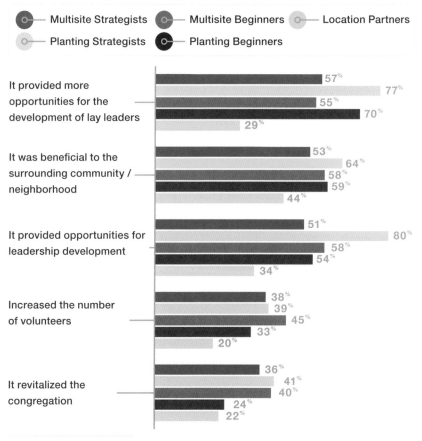

Positive Impact of Expansion on Church's Culture: Part 1

- Multisite Strategists
- Multisite Beginners
- Location Partners
- Planting Strategists
- Planting Beginners

It provided more opportunities for the development of lay leaders
- 57%
- 77%
- 55%
- 70%
- 29%

It was beneficial to the surrounding community / neighborhood
- 53%
- 64%
- 58%
- 59%
- 44%

It provided opportunities for leadership development
- 51%
- 80%
- 58%
- 54%
- 34%

Increased the number of volunteers
- 38%
- 39%
- 45%
- 33%
- 20%

It revitalized the congregation
- 36%
- 41%
- 40%
- 24%
- 22%

March 7–April 6, 2016, N=222.

Returning to Life Baptist Church in Las Vegas, Paul Gotthardt shares such an experience: "Going multisite allowed people who hadn't previously stepped up as leaders to fill the new, now vacant roles as they became open. Everyone on staff takes on a little bit more responsibility. It's taken us back to a narrative of God-dependence because we sent one-fifth of our funding out the door with that campus."

As we will see in a later chapter of *More Than Multisite*, the mother church of multisite campuses often provides more operational resources and support than church plants receive from their sending church. The latter, which tend to operate more autonomously, often rely more heavily on a deeply involved lay team. Yes, starting a new location revitalizes members and develops new leaders—but it can also wear on the launch team.

Starting a new location revitalizes members and develops new leaders—but it can also wear on the launch team

Most new churches, whether multisites or church plants, launch with a thin team. On average, new locations are led by one pastor, one part-time staff member and 12 volunteers from the congregation. Eight out of 10 leaders say their church launched with just one pastor, while the number of other staff varies (a majority lists one, two or no part-time employees and one or no full-time employees). However, some churches report up to a dozen pastors and staff and up to 200 volunteers. Eighteen percent—usually from much larger churches—say they also used a consultant to go multisite or plant.

Despite typically small launch teams, one-third of churches (32%) had "plenty" of staff and volunteers, and another one-third (32%) say it was "enough to get by." Only 13 percent say they definitely needed more people on the launch team.

As Barna has found in other research among church planters, a shared vision can be a galvanizing force, sustaining launch teams for many months or more. Furthermore, a clear vision can mobilize the surrounding community. Jodi Hickerson, a teaching pastor and programming director at Mission Church in Ventura, California, offers this encouragement: "You are going to need help. Have partners and churches willing to partner with you, even outside of fundraising. You need to depend on people."

Was the Launch Team Big Enough?

- **13%**
- **23%**
- **32%**
- **32%**

- Yes, we had plenty
- Kind of; we could get by
- No, we needed more
- Not sure

March 7–April 6, 2016, N=174 pastors of one church or campus.

When it comes to the downsides of expansion, negative effects include a revelation of leadership gaps (23%) and burdening staff or volunteers (12%). One in eight also says the spread of their ministry created division within their congregation or made it difficult to maintain alignment on mission. While all of these effects are relatively consistent across multisite and church plant types, Multisite Beginners are more likely to mention division within the congregation, which suggests that the move to open a new campus can be emotionally challenging for a church that has only recently adopted a multisite expansion strategy.

Negative Impact of Expansion on Church's Culture

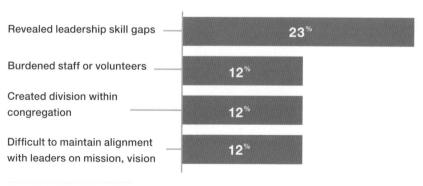

- Revealed leadership skill gaps — **23%**
- Burdened staff or volunteers — **12%**
- Created division within congregation — **12%**
- Difficult to maintain alignment with leaders on mission, vision — **12%**

March 7–April 6, 2016, N=222.

Numerical & Spiritual Growth

Surprisingly, a less commonly mentioned effect of church expansion is growth. Thirty percent say opening a new church or campus created new or increased growth, and 20 percent say it accelerated their pace of growth.

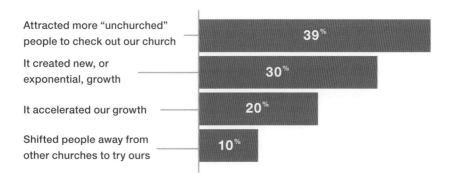

Impact of Expansion on Numerical Growth

Attracted more "unchurched" people to check out our church — **39%**

It created new, or exponential, growth — **30%**

It accelerated our growth — **20%**

Shifted people away from other churches to try ours — **10%**

March 7–April 6, 2016, N=222.

However, about two in five church leaders believe launching a new church or campus attracted more unchurched people than they might have seen at their sending church (39%). This is an important dynamic that many church leaders cite as a key reason for adding a location, rather than just growing an existing one: Many believe a church that is *new* and *local* is far more likely to attract new unchurched visitors than one that has been around for years.

Beyond numerical growth, researchers wondered about the *spiritual* growth of *existing* members. Having observed the challenges larger churches often face trying to engage members in discipleship programs, Barna hypothesized that launching a new church or campus and creating a smaller, more intimate environment might help to overcome such challenges.

Many leaders believe a *new* and *local* church is far more likely to attract unchurched visitors than one that has been around for years

Indeed, many churches using various growth strategies confirm that launching a new location fostered increased discipleship. Slightly less than half of church planters (45% Strategists, 39% Beginners) observed growth in discipleship, while somewhat fewer multisite churches report growth in this area (21% Strategists, 32% Beginners).

To get the fullest possible picture, researchers also asked if the effort of launching a new church *hindered* discipleship. Only 2 percent of churches report this effect.

Positive Impact of Expansion on Church's Culture: Part 2

Multisite Strategists · Multisite Beginners · Location Partners
Planting Strategists · Planting Beginners

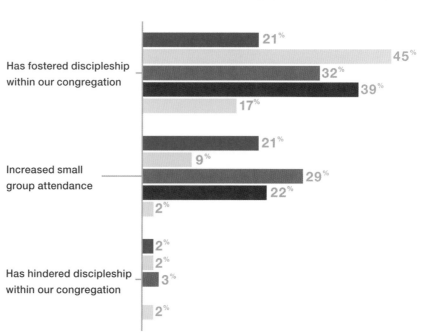

Has fostered discipleship within our congregation
- 21%
- 45%
- 32%
- 39%
- 17%

Increased small group attendance
- 21%
- 9%
- 29%
- 22%
- 2%

Has hindered discipleship within our congregation
- 2%
- 2%
- 3%
- 2%

March 7–April 6, 2016, *N*=222.

Reported changes in small group attendance are less consistent overall, likely due to the diversity of programs offered by different churches. However, on balance, approximately two out of 10 churches witness a growth in small group attendance as a result of opening a new campus or church.

Statistically and anecdotally, it appears that existing church members become more engaged, spiritually and in service, in a newer, smaller church in which they share a mission to their community.

Church members become more engaged, spiritually and in service, in a newer, smaller church in which they share a mission to their community

Dave Travis

Dave Travis is the Chief Executive Officer and Chief Encouragement Officer of Leadership Network, leading a large field team that works with innovative churches and ministries across the U.S. and Canada. Previously, he was a denominational leader, a pastor, a church staff member, an engineer and a consultant on church growth and development. He is coauthor of three books: *Beyond the Box*, *Beyond Megachurch Myths* and *What's Next*. Dave is a graduate of Georgia Institute of Technology and Southern Baptist Theological Seminary. He lives outside Atlanta, Georgia, with his wife, Lynne, and two daughters.

10 Trends of the Multisite Movement

By Dave Travis, Leadership Network

I was present at the beginning of this era of multisite ministry. It was an accident; I was just fortunate enough to work at Leadership Network at a time when we were making a list of and tracking the early practitioners of multisite. After a meeting with a church in 1997 that had already gone multisite, my team and I looked at each other and said, "This is going to be big."

We then saw a cadre of churches doing similar things across various geographic areas and denominational backgrounds. What began as a list of 78 in the '90s has grown to over 8,000, according to a Duke University survey.

I believe we are still in the early chapters of this story. There has been a rapid replication of sites and systems to fit the current context, but we are a long way from seeing the totality of this movement.

Drawing from the research within this report and my experience, here are some trends I have observed during the rise of expansion strategies, as well as a few shifts I think we have yet to see unfold.

1. From Thinking "Mega" to Thinking "Multi"

Twenty years ago when I came to work with larger churches, it was a point of pride for pastors to talk about the number of seats filled or the size of the venue. Now, most younger leaders focus on how to start additional sites and turn additional seats. Both strategies are derived from a desire to have greater impact in a region, but we see this multiplication perspective spreading.

2. The Big Four (or More)

There's a joke about how, when parents have more than two children, they have to move from one-on-one defense to zone defense. This could also apply to churches that exceed four campuses, a milestone at which relationships and communication really become complex. Of course, church staff relations and communications always have the potential to get messy, but especially with location dispersion.

3. "Aquimergertakeover" = Acquisition + Merger + Takeover

I hate to see sacred spaces sold to developers, and the "aquimergertakeover" is one solution. This idea is best described by Dr. Warren Bird and Jim Tomberlin in their book *Better Together*. I don't think there is a week when I don't read a story of an older congregation giving themselves and their property to a larger, healthier growing church. This is a way to establish strong congregations quickly into communities.

4. Suburban to Urban to Rural

I'm encouraged to see that many growing suburban churches are planting sites in urban places, closer to the center of their regional cities. Part of this is driven by the housing patterns of younger adults in those regions. Those successful in this approach are tailoring sites to these communities, and many use existing facilities in the city.

We're also seeing expansion from suburban to rural areas, something documented in the 2013 Leadership Network Generis Multisite Church Scorecard: "Another big surprise of the survey was how many churches (47%) have a campus in a small town or rural area. A Montana church opened its first multisite location in a rural location instead of in a larger city. A Texas congregation is reaching into multiple small towns, because there aren't any large cities within a three-hour drive. A North Carolina multisite leader notes: 'We are reaching people in smaller markets and rural areas outside large cities.'"

5. The Video-Driven Multisite Myth

The growth edge is in live teaching and preaching, not in video approaches. I believe the live teaching model that focuses on developing multiple preaching and teaching pastors is the new way to cultivate effective communicators for the future. For the teaching quality to remain high, there has to be continuous coaching, teamwork and development. This evolution of the teaching team model is to be applauded.

The live teaching model that focuses on developing multiple preaching and teaching pastors is the new way to cultivate effective communicators for the future

6. The Genius of Both / And

Some congregations are thinking about reproducing with both new sites and independent plants. They have different mindsets and models. Often, sites are established in a region where the team can still get together every week, while plants are more ideal for a distant geography. More churches are also launching planting networks to multiply contextual gospel communities. In some cases, the campus pastors and planters may be trained at "home base" and then deployed based on their gifts and calling. Regardless, the congregation has become the base initiator, not just a denominational entity.

7. Waiting on the Long-Term Plan

On a related note, what you start with is rarely what you end up with. Some sites spin off as independent; some stay as sites. The initiating pastor of the multisite vision may naturally make a transition. Sometimes I call the multisite strategy "church planting on the installment plan."

8. Increasing Lay Involvement

The tools used to launch a site deploy people who were previously not engaged. Typically, a matrix or grid is developed with all the "slots" for people to fill at a new campus. Once a certain percentage of these positions are filled, the site plan moves to the next stage. This creates "owners" of the new site early on and encourages those who like to pioneer new things.

9. Potential Growth Areas

I could see more churches establishing tailored venues on multiple sites that include multiple congregations, languages and musical styles. In addition, there are ample opportunities for churches to expand to institutions such as prisons, active adult communities, and the like.

10. Next Up:
Online Campus Strategy

One of the healthiest ways to look at online opportunity is to make it the equivalent of a site, with investment and staffing according to those reached. Internet congregations need a multifaceted ministry, not just a broadcast worship service.

Leadership Network has been conducting multisite research since its inception as a method for church expansion. Learn about Leadership Network's multisite resources—including a scorecard, toolkit and books—at leadnet.org

4 Facilities

In more ways than one, the foundation of a growing church is the location.

We have seen how most church leaders are clear on their mission and calling to minister in a new community. However, some are less prepared for the logistics of finding or building a suitable location or facility, and for the costs associated with this critical step in their mission. Approximately one out of 10 Beginners say finding a location was harder and more expensive than they imagined; this percentage nearly doubles among larger Strategist churches.

In qualitative research, leaders of large multisite church networks explain how the level of complexity, specificity of need and related costs go up with each additional new location. In the beginning, many are happy to make do with any sort of facility. As a church grows both in size

Impact of Expansion on Church's Facilities

Legend: Multisite Strategists — Multisite Beginners — Location Partners — Planting Strategists — Planting Beginners

Was more difficult than we imagined when it came to finding location(s)
- 19%
- 18%
- 11%
- 11%
- 10%

Was more expensive than we imagined
- 19%
- 18%
- 13%
- 9%
- 2%

March 7–April 6, 2016, N=222.

and reputation, however, a higher standard of quality is expected. Thus, along with higher expectations, the time and costs involved in finding and developing the optimal facility also grow.

Facility Choices & Needs

What are the essential needs of a multisite or planting church when it comes to facilities?

To help church leaders narrow down their priorities to the essentials, researchers asked them to choose what is *most important* to invest in if they were to face budget constraints. The findings clearly reveal that children's (and, to a lesser degree, youth) ministry areas are a top priority for all types of expanding churches.

Church plants (84% Strategists, 76% Beginners) most highly prioritize children's ministry spaces, suggesting that many of these communities tend to attract and serve young families. Multisite churches

Children's ministry areas are a top priority for all types of expanding churches

Top Two Facility Priorities

— Multisite Strategists   — Multisite Beginners   — Location Partners
— Planting Strategists   — Planting Beginners

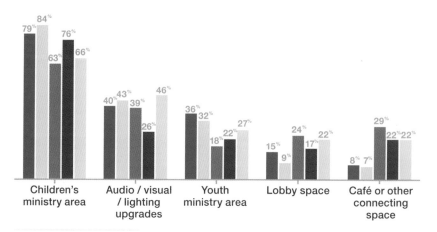

March 7–April 6, 2016, *N*=222.

(79% Strategists, 63% Beginners) also count children's ministry as their number-one priority, albeit by a slightly narrower margin.

Audio / visual capabilities and lighting are also an important investment. This is especially true for multisite churches, some of which rely on broadcasts or videos from related churches to deliver sermons or other community information. Four out of 10 multisite churches overall prioritize these technical aspects, with slightly fewer church plants selecting this option.

Given the importance of reaching and welcoming new visitors, researchers expected churches to place a high priority on gathering spaces such as the lobby or a café. Instead, just one in four Beginners see these as critically important, and even fewer Strategists consider them worth prioritizing if they faced budget constraints. This is not to say that churches do not invest at all in these features, but to emphasize that children's and youth ministry spaces (and, to a lesser degree, technology and lighting) are seen as more critical than spaces set aside for fellowship and community. This finding fits comfortably with other results that show the premium leaders place on children's ministry to attract and minister to young families.

Facility Trade-Offs

The research team decided to "pressure test" growing churches' facility-related choices to determine their priorities. Trade-off questions helped to zero-in on what's most important when it comes to their physical space and location.

First, how flexible are churches in their choice of facility? Multisite campuses and co-located congregations are somewhat more likely to say a *purpose-built* church—one designed and built specifically to be a church, not converted from another type of space—is their preference, compared to church plants, which more often "can make any type of space work."

Purpose-Built Church vs. Any Type of Space

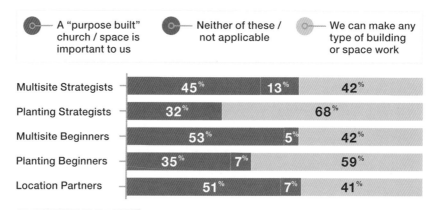

A "purpose built" church / space is important to us — **Neither of these / not applicable** — **We can make any type of building or space work**

Multisite Strategists	45%	13%	42%
Planting Strategists	32%		68%
Multisite Beginners	53%	5%	42%
Planting Beginners	35%	7%	59%
Location Partners	51%	7%	41%

March 7–April 6, 2016, *N*=222.

Faced with the trade-off between location and size of space, respondents indicate that *location* is significantly more important, particularly for Planting Strategists (77%).

Frank Wooden, director of church multiplication for Southern California Assemblies of God, also serves as lead pastor for San Diego

Ideal Location vs. Size of Space

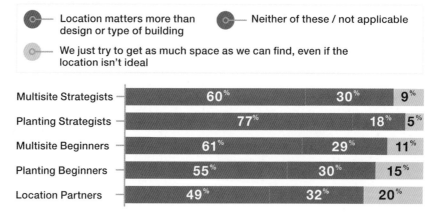

Location matters more than design or type of building — **Neither of these / not applicable**

We just try to get as much space as we can find, even if the location isn't ideal

Multisite Strategists	60%	30%	9%
Planting Strategists	77%	18%	5%
Multisite Beginners	61%	29%	11%
Planting Beginners	55%	30%	15%
Location Partners	49%	32%	20%

March 7–April 6, 2016, *N*=222.

Hope Church. Location has played a pivotal role in their facilities choices: "We found the center of the neighborhoods where we were looking, where the hub of life was. Then we planted within half a block of those spots. You can compromise some on the facility to stay true to the location / demographic you're trying to reach."

Pastors are split on the importance of managing costs versus investing in aesthetic design. Under the assumption that good design attracts people to the church, look and feel seems to be somewhat more important to multisite churches than to church plants.

Furthermore, Barna and CKN's previous research with Millennials (born 1984 or later) reveals that the youngest adult generation highly values good design and a sense of place. Many Millennials are drawn to traditional churches. They also tend to prize local facilities that are tailored to their unique context. This lends support to the current multisite and church plant leaders' bias toward quality facility design, but also suggests that greater investment in aesthetics could make a difference in attracting Millennials.

Design Aesthetics vs. Cost

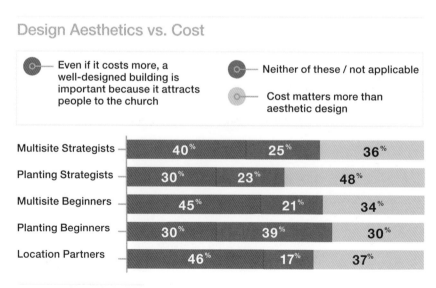

March 7–April 6, 2016, N=222.

When it comes to functional design, churches are reluctant to cut corners

When it comes to *functional* design, as opposed to aesthetics, churches are reluctant to cut corners. Investing in this type of design means thinking through the ways a facility can help operations run more smoothly: How do people get in and out of the building? How does this flow align with the order of service? Is there ample support space for technical needs (such as lighting and audio / visual equipment)? Where can people meet and connect without interfering with other ministry spaces? Preference for good functional design is particularly strong among Multisite Beginners (74%).

Rob Cizek, executive pastor of Northshore Christian Church in Everett, Washington, cautions, "If you can't afford it all at once, build half and lay groundwork for a phase two. Don't get trapped in planning only for what you need now. Take the extra time to get the input from all the people who will be using the space, to build space that people really want to be in and use."

Design Function vs. Cost

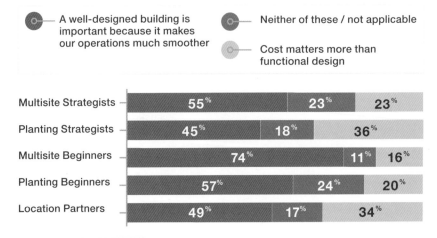

○ A well-designed building is important because it makes our operations much smoother

○ Neither of these / not applicable

○ Cost matters more than functional design

Multisite Strategists	55%	23%	23%
Planting Strategists	45%	18%	36%
Multisite Beginners	74%	11%	16%
Planting Beginners	57%	24%	20%
Location Partners	49%	17%	34%

March 7–April 6, 2016, *N*=222.

Most churches of all types desire a permanent facility rather than a flexible, temporary space. Lead pastor Mike Hickerson explains why he prefers permanency for his own ministry, Mission Church in Ventura, California. "I think there's something awesome when a church says, 'We're not portable; we're putting roots down in the city. We're here, we're invested.' I'd love to see a community center, for the church to be used more than just on Sunday; for a church to be a lighthouse for the community; for people to say 'I don't know if I believe what they believe, but man, they offer a lot of hope to our city.'"

A significant minority of church plants believes a permanent facility might constrain their growth (22% Beginners). This finding was somewhat unexpected, given that many church plants do, in fact, operate within a temporary space, most often a school. About one-third of all church types rent their current facilities, but most seem to agree on the ideal: a permanent facility, in a good location, designed to optimize operations.

Permanent vs. Temporary

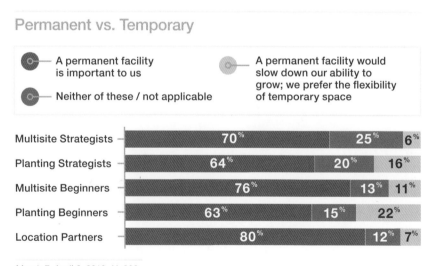

March 7–April 6, 2016, *N*=222.

Any discussion of church facilities must also include office space. Where does the church staff work during "the rest of the week?" For multisite churches, offices are most often in a central location, usually at the main church, but sometimes elsewhere. Just over half of church plants have offices at their individual church, but the balance use shared office space, leveraging their network both for efficiencies in facility management and for resource-sharing.

Location of Office Space

At individual campuses   At another location   At the main church

	Multisite Strategists	Planting Strategists	Multisite Beginners	Planting Beginners
At individual campuses	76%	41%	55%	41%
At another location	4%	6%	13%	2%
At the main church	20%	52%	32%	56%

March 7–April 6, 2016, N=222.

Financing

Barna Group, in partnership with Thrivent Financial, conducted a survey of church planters and their finances in 2014. The study found that many planters put themselves under personal financial strain, which often leads to stressors in their family life, in order to keep the new church afloat when income is low. With those findings as background, researchers naturally wondered about the financial condition of the campuses and churches in the *More Than Multisite* study.

Many church planters put themselves under personal financial strain in order to keep the new church afloat

How do churches prepare financially for future growth? They rely on a variety of strategies for raising needed funds. Church plants are most likely to be organically self-funding—that is, giving increases as they grow, and those funds covers increasing operational expenses. Nearly three-quarters of Planting Beginners (72%) say they primarily rely on this approach. Meanwhile, two-thirds of Planting Strategists (66%) also use this self-funding approach, but half (48%) say they also set aside a certain percentage of their operating budget for ongoing growth, since their expansion strategy specifically includes continued growth and regeneration.

Roughly one-quarter of Planting Beginners report they raise funds when they need them (26%) or have capital campaigns (20%). Planting Strategists, on the other hand, are least likely to wait until funds are needed to begin raising them (14%).

Planning for Future Growth

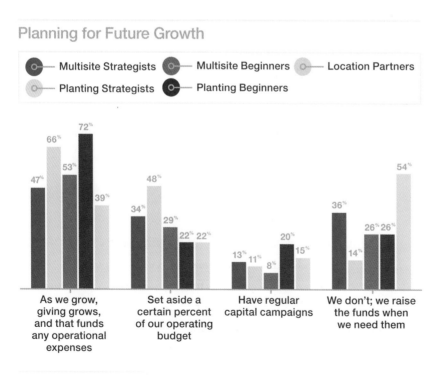

● — Multisite Strategists ○ — Multisite Beginners ○ — Location Partners
○ — Planting Strategists ● — Planting Beginners

March 7–April 6, 2016, N=222.

Interestingly, more than one-third of Multisite Strategists (36%) say they do not raise funds for growth in advance; they wait until they need them. It may be that the size of these church networks and the number of congregants they are able to rely on enables them to take this as-needed approach. A similar proportion of Multisite Strategists (34%) set aside a percentage of their operating budget for future growth, and nearly half rely on organic growth from increased giving.

Location Partners, which tend to have a less intentional growth strategy, most commonly raise funds as needed (54%) or say this question is not applicable to them (7%). However, more than one-third are proactive about raising funds for growth: 22 percent set aside operating budget and 15 percent conduct capital campaigns.

How do churches rely on their network or sending church when it comes to financial matters—if they do at all? Church plants are most likely to operate completely or partially independently, with only 17 percent of Planting Beginners sharing all financial decisions with their sending church(es). Planting Strategists operate in a more coordinated way, with one-quarter saying financial decisions are completely centralized (27%).

Finances / Budget: Centralized or Decentralized?

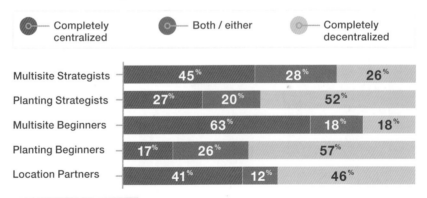

March 7–April 6, 2016, N=222.

Multisites, however, tend to take the opposite approach. Among this network, Beginners have very close ties to the mother church; nearly two-thirds say financial decisions are completely centralized (63%). Slightly fewer Multisite Strategists have centralized budgeting processes (45%)—though still significantly more than church plants. Location Partners are a mix.

When budgets are centrally coordinated, how are new church locations funded? Financial allocations are most commonly made according to need (45%), or churches start out self-sufficient (31%). A minority of churches allocates based on campus size (16%), a set percentage of a church network budget (12%) or of the campus income (7%). These allocations are mostly perceived as equitable—more than half (55%) say they are "definitely" fair, while 40 percent believe they are "somewhat" fair, which may indicate some latent dissatisfaction.

Financial allocations for new church locations are most commonly made according to need, and more than half perceive the allocations are fair

How Churches Allocate Funds Across Campuses

% among churches with centralized finances

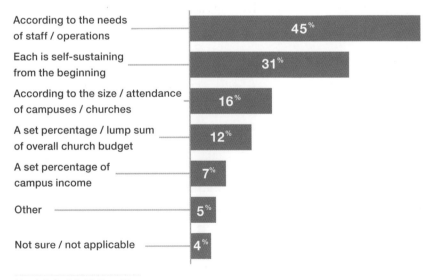

According to the needs of staff / operations	45%
Each is self-sustaining from the beginning	31%
According to the size / attendance of campuses / churches	16%
A set percentage / lump sum of overall church budget	12%
A set percentage of campus income	7%
Other	5%
Not sure / not applicable	4%

March 7–April 6, 2016, *n*=85.

Built to Grow

The physical dimensions of adding a congregation

We've established that each model of church growth has its own unique views on building and investing in ministry facilities. How do their strategies compare to those of all expanding churches combined?

More than half of all actively expanding churches are most concerned with the location or functional design of their building

A permanent facility is very important to us — **70%**

Good design matters to attract people — **38%**

Location matters more than design or type of building — **60%**

Cost matters more than aesthetic design — **37%**

Good design matters for smoother operations — **55%**

Cost matters more than functional design — **26%**

We can make any space work — **51%**

We just try to get as much space as we can find, even if the location isn't ideal — **12%**

A purpose-built church is very important — **43%**

We prefer the flexibility of temporary space — **12%**

A Fixed Spot

Permanency is seen as vital, no matter what a church's philosophy of facilities may be.

88%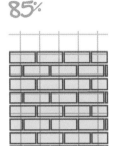

of those who value a purpose-built church

85%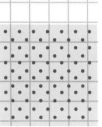

of those who value a well-designed building to attract people

80%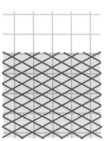

of those who value a well-designed building to make operations smoother

67%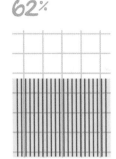

of those who value location more than design

62%

of those who value cost more than aesthetics

% among all rapidly expanding churches

Facilities with a Mission

How does a church's ministry strategy affect their building decisions? Churches that are expanding to better reach a community to which they feel called typically place greater emphasis on having a well-designed building. Meanwhile, ministries that are fulfilling a specific strategy are more cost-conscious in their building efforts.

 Churches reproducing to be more effective in reaching our city/region

 Churches reproducing to fulfill our mission/strategic plan

Even if it costs more, a well-designed building is important because …

it attracts people to the church

 47%   31%

it makes operations smoother

 65%   53%

Cost matters more than …

aesthetic design

 51%   31%

functional design

 36%   18%

Facility Decisions & Experiences

To get a better sense of the facility decisions that face multisite and church plants, researchers asked pastors of a single campus or church (a total of 157 respondents) to elaborate on the facilities they have previously used and are currently using.

Where They Moved

First, one-third of churches launched in a purpose-built church building (32%). The research team was surprised by the number of campuses and churches that first opened in such a space, though some of these may well have been older churches repurposed for a new congregation. Temporary or transitional space (usually schools) was the next most common situation at 24 percent, followed by a renovated existing church building (18%). Beyond this, churches met in a wide range of location types.

More than half of churches moved into a new, custom-built facility, with another 28 percent making some sort of renovations to a previously used or build-to-suit space.

First Facility Was . . .

% among pastors of a single campus / church

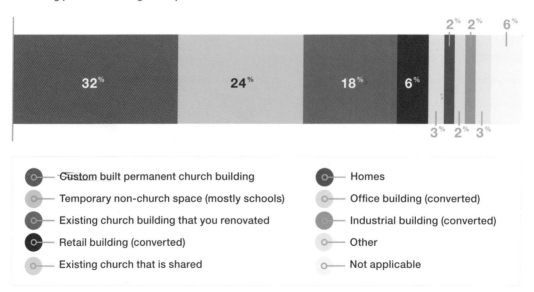

- Custom built permanent church building — 32%
- Temporary non-church space (mostly schools) — 24%
- Existing church building that you renovated — 18%
- Retail building (converted) — 6%
- Existing church that is shared — 3%
- Homes — 2%
- Office building (converted) — 2%
- Industrial building (converted) — 3%
- Other — 2%
- Not applicable — 6%

March 7–April 6, 2016, *n*=157.

First Facility's Condition Was . . .

% among pastors of a single campus / church

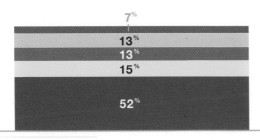

- 7%
- 13%
- 13%
- 15%
- 52%

Legend:
- Other, N / A
- Used / no renovations
- Used / minor renovations
- Used / major renovations
- New / custom built

March 7–April 6, 2016, *n*=157.

Why They Moved

Thinking next about their move into the facility where their church meets today, leaders were asked about their decisions and preparations. Needing to find their first permanent space or outgrowing capacity were top reasons to move to their current location, followed by a desire to reach out to a certain neighborhood. This missional motivation reflects what researchers heard from several church planters and multisite leaders in the qualitative research.

Reasons for Move to Current Facility

% among pastors of a single campus / church

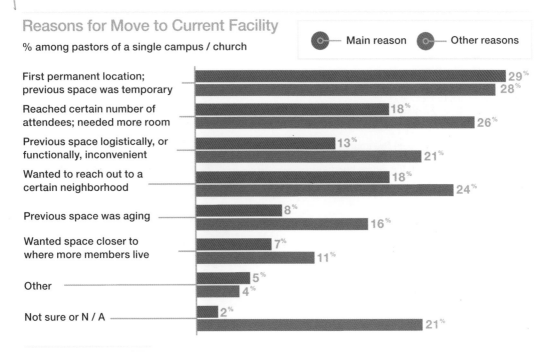

Legend: Main reason — Other reasons

Reason	Main reason	Other reasons
First permanent location; previous space was temporary	29%	28%
Reached certain number of attendees; needed more room	18%	26%
Previous space logistically, or functionally, inconvenient	13%	21%
Wanted to reach out to a certain neighborhood	18%	24%
Previous space was aging	8%	16%
Wanted space closer to where more members live	7%	11%
Other	5%	4%
Not sure or N / A	2%	21%

March 7–April 6, 2016, *n*=157.

The Costs of a New Facility

The majority of the new (or renovated) facilities cost less than $1 million, including purchase price, renovation and mortgage, when applicable. To level this cost across geographic locations, churches divided this by their annual operating budget. On average, the cost of a new facility represented about two-and-a-half times the church's annual budget (median 250%).

Total Cost of New Facility

% among pastors of a single campus / church

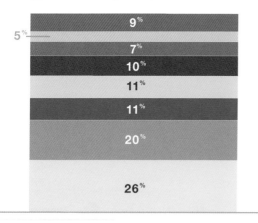

March 7–April 6, 2016, n=99.

Funding & Financing the New Facility

% among pastors of a single campus / church

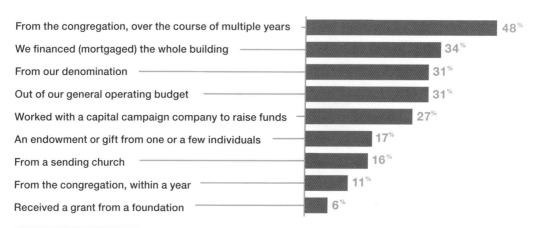

From the congregation, over the course of multiple years	48%
We financed (mortgaged) the whole building	34%
From our denomination	31%
Out of our general operating budget	31%
Worked with a capital campaign company to raise funds	27%
An endowment or gift from one or a few individuals	17%
From a sending church	16%
From the congregation, within a year	11%
Received a grant from a foundation	6%

March 7–April 6, 2016, n=99.

More Than Multisite

About half raised funds for their move over the course of multiple years (only 11% completed fundraising within one year). One-third of churches also drew from their annual operating budget or received funds from their denomination. One-third fully mortgaged the entire building.

Lessons Learned

What did churches learn from their experience of finding, designing and moving into a new facility? Most cite lessons about improved effectiveness in outreach as a result of thoughtful building design. For example, four in 10 say choosing a traditional church building gave them credibility in their community. Some of the in-depth interviews revealed a similar theme: This is an intentional strategy of Christ the King in Boston, Massachusetts, for example, and one reason why some churches chose to merge with older, dwindling churches.

Another two in 10 point to these benefits of intentional design:

- Tailoring the facility to a certain demographic (for example, having family-friendly facilities such as larger bathrooms or designated children's spaces) helped the church reach that group more effectively
- Investing in good design helped to attract newcomers in general
- Being a part of physically restoring a neighborhood has built a strong sense of trust and openness in a new community

Experiences / Lessons from Current Facility

% among pastors of a single campus / church

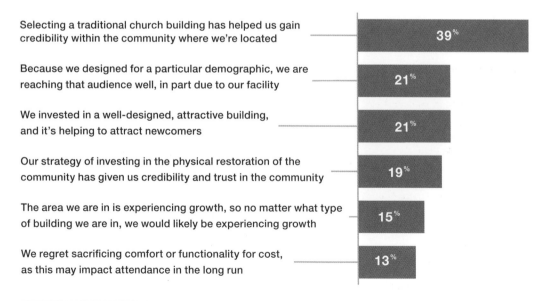

Selecting a traditional church building has helped us gain credibility within the community where we're located — 39%

Because we designed for a particular demographic, we are reaching that audience well, in part due to our facility — 21%

We invested in a well-designed, attractive building, and it's helping to attract newcomers — 21%

Our strategy of investing in the physical restoration of the community has given us credibility and trust in the community — 19%

The area we are in is experiencing growth, so no matter what type of building we are in, we would likely be experiencing growth — 15%

We regret sacrificing comfort or functionality for cost, as this may impact attendance in the long run — 13%

March 7–April 6, 2016, *n*=99.

These lessons suggest that thoughtful, intentional building design is very much on-strategy. And because these multisite churches and church plants are so mission-driven, the right space is a sound investment in what they feel God has clearly called them to do.

At the same time, many offer advice for what they would do differently if they could do their move over again:

- **Build bigger** and **plan for more growth** (echoed by in-depth interviews)*
- Specifically, churches often say they would **build more and larger classrooms**, especially for kids and youth ministries
- **Plan better** with a more **intentional design** for their specific needs
- More carefully **plan out operational costs** (for example, high sanctuary ceilings are difficult to heat and cool)
- Planting churches also say they would **select a better location** in the community for their church
- Some multisite churches say they would **consider access issues** (handicap accessibility, access from the road and parking) more carefully

---

* In addition to many pastors explicitly stating they wish they had planned for more space, reported financing of new spaces reveals that many raise funds according to their current size rather than future growth. If a church is still growing, by the time a building project is completed, they will quickly expand beyond the size planned for during fundraising.

5 Leadership, Pastors & Preaching

The introduction of *More Than Multisite* suggests this principle: Leadership is a key determinant of the pace and model of growth. Pastors in the in-depth interviews explained how the emergence of a leader is often the catalyst for a new church plant or campus, often in a certain area where God is clearly calling that leader. On the other hand, according to the national survey, the most common negative impact of expansion is that it reveals leadership gaps. Leadership, then, is a critical topic to explore when it comes to understanding how churches grow.

Most churches in the study have two full-time pastors and between one and three part-time pastors, with Multisite and Planting Strategists on the higher end of these averages.

Leadership is a key determinant of the pace and model of growth

Median Number of Full-Time and Part-Time Pastors

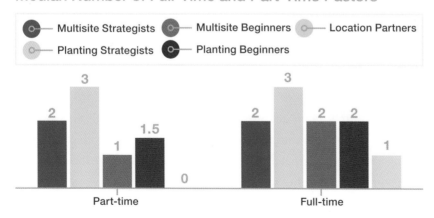

March 7–April 6, 2016, *N*=222.

When adjusting for congregation size, however, we find that many pastors are stretched thin, with about half of all churches having one pastor per 100 congregants. This is especially true of Multisite Beginners, 60 percent of whom have just one pastor for more than 100 parishioners. Multisite Strategists and Location Partners, on the other hand, are more likely to have a lower pastor-to-congregant ratio. Both of these likely enjoy more centralized leadership support than planting churches and churches in the early stages of a multisite expansion.

Number of Pastors per 100 Congregants

Legend: Multisite Strategists · Multisite Beginners · Location Partners · Planting Strategists · Planting Beginners

1 pastor to <100 congregants: 60%, 50%, 40%, 50%, 60%

1 pastor to 100+ congregants: 40%, 50%, 60%, 50%, 40%

March 7–April 6, 2016, N=222.

When people think about a multisite church, many picture a televised message. While this is true for a small number of campuses, it is not the norm

What role do these pastors play? When people think about a multisite church, many picture a televised message. While this is true for a small number of campuses, it is not the norm. Across church types, having a dedicated campus pastor who preaches a message locally is the most common preaching scenario and seems to be the most satisfactory approach.

"In the long run, the church will do better if we keep raising up communicators," says Tom Hughes of Christian Assembly in Los Angeles. "While we use video within our multi-venue campus, the church plants we support do not use video teaching. It forces us to keep identifying and developing younger communicators . . . to be able to contextualize the gospel into the particular neighborhood of the church plant."

A shared pastor who travels between campuses is the next most common approach, which is particularly popular among Multisite Beginners (37%). The shared-pastor model becomes increasingly complicated as the number of churches or campuses grows, so this approach is only seen in about one in eight Multisite Strategist churches (13%). Additionally, three out of 10 churches that use this approach say it needs improvement.

A televised sermon, whether live or pre-recorded, is used by fewer than one in 10 Multisites and Planting Strategists. Pastors say the live broadcast approach is a challenge; one out of five says it needs improvement, and another three in five say it "works okay." Multisite pastors in the qualitative interviews said the same: The risk of technical glitches with a live broadcast is too high, and many quickly switched from live to a pre-recorded message. Those who use a pre-recorded sermon report much higher satisfaction (four out of five say it "works great").

"There is no culture creator like the pulpit, so having video feed helps keep the culture consistent," says Joby Martin, founding and lead pastor of The Church of Eleven22 in Jacksonville, Florida. But, he acknowledges, there can be negative perceptions until people attend a video venue and experience that it is not just an overflow of the main campus, but rather an additional campus that loves and serves its congregation, neighbors and community.

Preaching in Church Network

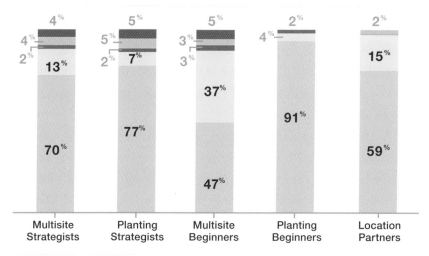

- The sermon is pre-recorded and played later
- The sermon is broadcast live
- A team of pastors rotates around sites
- There is a shared pastor (who travels around)
- Each campus has its own pastor

March 7–April 6, 2016, N=222.

Success of Preaching Approach

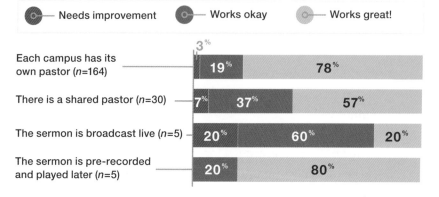

- Needs improvement
- Works okay
- Works great!

Each campus has its own pastor (n=164) — 3% / 19% / 78%

There is a shared pastor (n=30) — 7% / 37% / 57%

The sermon is broadcast live (n=5) — 20% / 60% / 20%

The sermon is pre-recorded and played later (n=5) — 20% / 80%

March 7–April 6, 2016, N=204.

Pastoral Relationships & Support

Knowing that disagreements among leaders can deeply impact a growing church, researchers pressed pastors on interpersonal dynamics and logistical stressors.

Among those who lead a single campus or church, only one out of 20 says they feel insufficiently supported by their church network. The majority expresses very few underlying concerns about their leadership model or their role. Only one out of 10 agrees with statements that suggest dissatisfaction with shared pastoral responsibilities, preaching or other leadership. In most cases, this is simply because this dynamic (sharing their role with another central pastor) is not common.

Pastors who oversee multiple campuses express more concerns, mainly around coordinating across sites and staff. One-quarter feel exhausted from juggling the needs of multiple locations and staffs. One out of five says it is difficult to maintain alignment on church mission and vision. Pastors in central roles relieve church and campus pastors so they can focus more on their pastoral duties, but as a consequence they take on much of the stress associated with an operational role.

Pastors who oversee multiple campuses express concerns around coordinating across sites and staff

"[There are challenges in the] relationship between central support (global) and campuses (specific), in finding the right balance between autonomy or freedom and central control. It's a dance, back and forth," says pastor Rick Langston of The Summit Church in Raleigh-Durham, North Carolina. "How much are we trying to ensure there's some uniformity in vision and execution . . . but doing it in such a way that we don't hinder or restrict gifts at a campus? Campus [leaders] are not drones. This is where frustration comes. We continually focus on communication and building healthy team relationships to minimize this tension."

Lead pastor Josh Surratt's experience with Seacoast Church in the Carolinas inspires his suggestions for unity in leadership: "We have to put language to values, cultural responsibilities that we have taken for granted. We must be more intentional, must protect our DNA."

Challenges to Pastors of Multiple Campuses
% among pastors of multiple campuses / churches

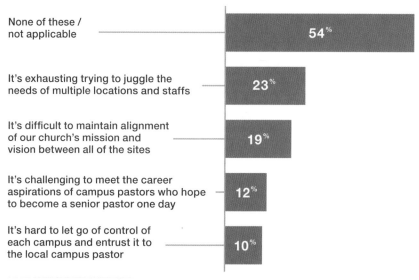

None of these /
not applicable — **54**%

It's exhausting trying to juggle the
needs of multiple locations and staffs — **23**%

It's difficult to maintain alignment
of our church's mission and
vision between all of the sites — **19**%

It's challenging to meet the career
aspirations of campus pastors who hope
to become a senior pastor one day — **12**%

It's hard to let go of control of
each campus and entrust it to
the local campus pastor — **10**%

March 7–April 6, 2016, n=98.

Previously in *More Than Multisite*, we looked at centralized versus autonomous decision-making with regard to identity and branding, and budgets and finances. In addition to these issues, Barna asked pastors about a range of leadership and operational factors to understand more about the leadership dynamics at work in and preferred by multisite and planting churches.

Not surprisingly, leadership of multisite churches is more centralized across all factors. However, a significant degree of centralized decision-making also takes place in planting churches.

In the general category of "leadership and ministry," about half of church plants report having complete autonomy, while the majority of multisite churches share responsibility. Multisite Beginners (42%) and Location Partners (39%) are most likely to have completely centralized leadership.

Leadership / Ministry: Centralized or Decentralized?

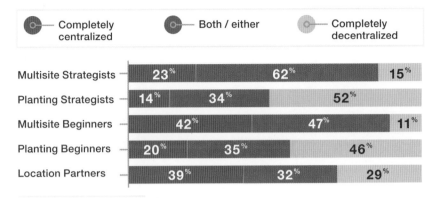

	Completely centralized	Both / either	Completely decentralized
Multisite Strategists	23%	62%	15%
Planting Strategists	14%	34%	52%
Multisite Beginners	42%	47%	11%
Planting Beginners	20%	35%	46%
Location Partners	39%	32%	29%

March 7–April 6, 2016, *N*=222.

With regard to governance through elders, more multisite churches report completely centralized leadership, while more church plants report more autonomy.

Elders: Centralized or Decentralized?

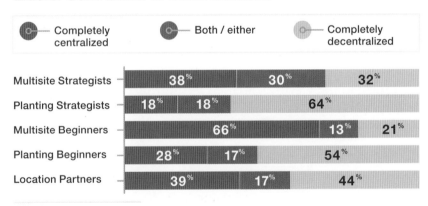

	Completely centralized	Both / either	Completely decentralized
Multisite Strategists	38%	30%	32%
Planting Strategists	18%	18%	64%
Multisite Beginners	66%	13%	21%
Planting Beginners	28%	17%	54%
Location Partners	39%	17%	44%

March 7–April 6, 2016, *N*=222.

When it comes to operations, there is more of a mix. Approximately one-third of most groups share responsibility for operations with a central network, while slightly more than half of church plants have autonomy in this area. Around one-third of multisites and co-located congregations have centralized operations.

Operational Roles: Centralized or Decentralized?

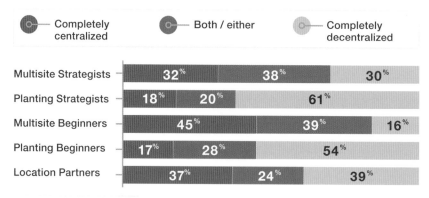

● — Completely centralized   ● — Both / either   ● — Completely decentralized

	Completely centralized	Both / either	Completely decentralized
Multisite Strategists	32%	38%	30%
Planting Strategists	18%	20%	61%
Multisite Beginners	45%	39%	16%
Planting Beginners	17%	28%	54%
Location Partners	37%	24%	39%

March 7–April 6, 2016, *N*=222.

Support functions, such as legal, human resources (HR), information technology (IT) and the like are significantly more likely than other roles and functions to be centralized. Half to two-thirds of multisite churches benefit from fully centralized support functions, and about one-third of church plants and co-located congregations also tap into central resources.

Support Roles: Centralized or Decentralized?

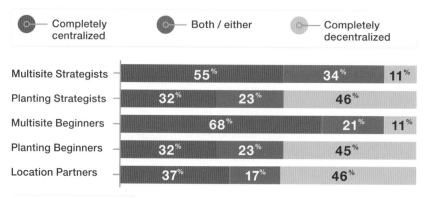

● — Completely centralized   ● — Both / either   ● — Completely decentralized

	Completely centralized	Both / either	Completely decentralized
Multisite Strategists	55%	34%	11%
Planting Strategists	32%	23%	46%
Multisite Beginners	68%	21%	11%
Planting Beginners	32%	23%	45%
Location Partners	37%	17%	46%

March 7–April 6, 2016, *N*=222.

Bob Sawyer

Bob Sawyer is the director of the Church Planting Center at Christ the King (CTK) Boston. Currently, CTK has eight congregations, with other projects in the works. The CTK Church Planting Center strategically builds up leaders and churches in the greater Boston area, neighborhood by neighborhood.

Q&A with Bob Sawyer: Leading Strategic Growth

Q: On Learning from Experienced Planting / Multisite Leaders

A: We went to San Diego to observe Harbor Presbyterian Church, a multisite church. Rick Downs (pastor of CTK Boston) caught the vision and did a sabbatical there to learn about it. A couple of years later, several other leaders went out there to study the model and came back enthusiastic about it.

Q: On Providing Support Functions for New Churches

A: We didn't want this to fall on the senior pastor and be a distraction. We knew we needed a dedicated resource with bandwidth, someone who is equipped for that work [such as operations, legal, finances, signing leases, etc.]. We provide stability. . . . We want to build something that's here for the next generation. The structure helps us take a long view of the city.

Q: On Identifying Locations & Leaders

A: Our desire is to continue planting under CTK, all under one session and one administrative infrastructure, but with local leaders. We are very neighborhood-focused. CTK wants to plant a church in every neighborhood in and around Boston. This is missional church planting. It's not about growth and needing to find a new facility; it's about viewing the city as a mission field and deploying people all around the city, hoping those churches will do the hard work of spreading the gospel.

Planters have to be willing to be a part of the CTK network. Some are developed from the inside, some come to us, some we go out to find. We stay plugged into networks to grow and maintain talent.

Q: On Connection & Collaboration Between Campus Pastors

A: Each pastor wears two hats: one for their local context and one for the CTK network. It's collegial; no renegade or autonomous leaders who want to do their own thing. There is a relational glue between pastors; they gather weekly on video conference to talk about preaching the same text and same schedule. They do this of their own will. It's organic; they want to be a part of the same thing. Very relational, not top-down.

Q: On the Future (and Past) of Church Expansion

A: What does the church gain by planting this way? We want to hold it very loosely; Jesus is still advancing his kingdom if this all goes away tomorrow. It's not like we've figured anything out; we're going with a strategic approach that seems a part of our call: to love the city we're familiar with. We need to treat it like they did according to Acts: treat all the places people live as places where we need to take the gospel. This enables us to avoid competing over territory, to build a support network, to create a unified sense of responsibility for the city as a whole.

6 Growing Forward

While the churches and leaders included in this study represent a wide variety of approaches to growth and reaching communities with the gospel, one thing is consistent: their calling and commitment to their vision. The diversity of these models and the communities in which they operate reflects the beautiful diversity of the universal Church itself.

There are *many* ways of expanding or reproducing a congregation, and this research suggests that there is a time, place and situation to which each of these models is suited. The thing to know is that churches *are* growing, and there are many who desire to make Christ known in every corner of their world. Their energy and vision create opportunities for leadership development, which in turn create more opportunities for discipleship and evangelism—a multiplying effect that is foundational to the spread of the gospel.

Barna and Cornerstone Knowledge Network are encouraged by these findings and pray they prove useful to the work of future leaders—people who hear and heed the call to build something new, whether it be congregation or a campus or a children's ministry. The logistics of building on a vision and seeing it come to fruition can be more complicated or consuming than many leaders imagine. With insights from those who have gone before and statistical analysis of their successes, we hope future leaders will find themselves better equipped to navigate critical, ministry-shaping decisions with awareness and understanding. It is our hope that more informed decision-making will translate to more intentional ministry design—leaving more time for pastors and leaders to focus on the great spiritual work they have been called to.

With insights from those who have gone before and statistical analysis of their successes, we hope future leaders will find themselves better equipped to navigate critical, ministry-shaping decisions

Appendix

A. Data Tables

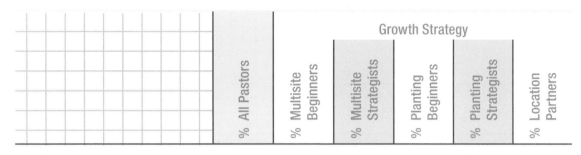

	% All Pastors	Growth Strategy				
		% Multisite Beginners	% Multisite Strategists	% Planting Beginners	% Planting Strategists	% Location Partners

Q1: What is your current age?

	% All Pastors	% Multisite Beginners	% Multisite Strategists	% Planting Beginners	% Planting Strategists	% Location Partners
18 to 50	49	55	50	41	55	46
51 and older	51	45	50	59	45	54

	% All Pastors	Growth Strategy				
		% Multisite Beginners	% Multisite Strategists	% Planting Beginners	% Planting Strategists	% Location Partners

Q2: Do you consider yourself to be...?

	% All Pastors	% Multisite Beginners	% Multisite Strategists	% Planting Beginners	% Planting Strategists	% Location Partners
White	89	97	81	98	77	95
Black / African American	4	3	6		7	2
Hispanic / Latino(a)	4		8	2	7	
Asian / Asian American	2		4		5	
Another ethnic group	2		2		5	2

	% All Pastors	% Multisite Beginners	Growth Strategy % Multisite Strategists	% Planting Beginners	% Planting Strategists	% Location Partners

Q3: Did you attend seminary?

	% All Pastors	% Multisite Beginners	% Multisite Strategists	% Planting Beginners	% Planting Strategists	% Location Partners
Yes, graduated	80	79	79	80	70	93
Yes, but did not graduate	8	3	8	11	14	5
No, did not attend	12	18	13	9	16	2

Q4: Is your position…?

	% All Pastors	% Multisite Beginners	% Multisite Strategists	% Planting Beginners	% Planting Strategists	% Location Partners
Full-time, paid	93	95	92	93	91	95
Part-time, paid	4	5	4	4	2	5
Full-time, volunteer	1		2		2	
Part-time, volunteer	1			2	5	
Other	0		2			

	% All Pastors	% Multisite Beginners	% Multisite Strategists	% Planting Beginners	% Planting Strategists	% Location Partners
			Growth Strategy			

Q5: What is your current role at your church?

	% All Pastors	% Multisite Beginners	% Multisite Strategists	% Planting Beginners	% Planting Strategists	% Location Partners
Senior Pastor / Minister	90	71	87	96	95	100
Executive Pastor / Director / Chief Operating Officer	5	13	8	4	2	
Church Campus Pastor / Minister	3	11	2		2	
Multisite Pastor / Director	1	3	4			
Associate Pastor / Minister		3				

		Growth Strategy			
All Pastors	Multisite Beginners	Multisite Strategists	Planting Beginners	Planting Strategists	Location Partners

Q6: How many years have you been in your current role?

Median	8	5	7	10	8 to 9	8

		Growth Strategy			
All Pastors	Multisite Beginners	Multisite Strategists	Planting Beginners	Planting Strategists	Location Partners

Q7: How many years have you been at your current church?

Median	8	6.5	6.5	10	9	6

	% All Pastors	% Multisite Beginners	Growth strategy			
			% Multisite Strategists	% Planting Beginners	% Planting Strategists	% Location Partners

Q8: Would you consider your church to be any of the following? Select one.

	% All Pastors	% Multisite Beginners	% Multisite Strategists	% Planting Beginners	% Planting Strategists	% Location Partners
A multisite church (one church with two or more geographical locations)	23	84	34			
A multisite church network (multiple campuses and affiliated churches)	6	16	13			
A "reproducing" church (duplicated campuses and/or church plants)	20			61	39	
A "multiplying" church (multiple campuses that have birthed campuses and/or church plants that have planted churches)	10			13	39	
A central organization responsible for supporting or managing a group of related churches	10			26	23	100
An individual congregation that is part of a larger church	31		53			

	% All Pastors	% Multisite Beginners	Growth strategy			% Location Partners
			% Multisite Strategists	% Planting Beginners	% Planting Strategists	

Q9: Does your responsibility cover one campus / church or multiple campuses / churches?

	% All Pastors	% Multisite Beginners	% Multisite Strategists	% Planting Beginners	% Planting Strategists	% Location Partners
I am responsible for ONE campus / church	56	21	55	67	52	80
I am responsible for MULTIPLE campuses / churches	44	79	45	33	48	20

	All Pastors	Multisite Beginners	Growth Strategy			Location Partners
			Multisite Strategists	Planting Beginners	Planting Strategists	

Q10: Currently, how many adults attend your church's worship services on a typical weekend at this site? (Among pastors of one campus or church.)

	All Pastors	Multisite Beginners	Multisite Strategists	Planting Beginners	Planting Strategists	Location Partners
Median	130	124	125	185 to 200	120	120 to 140

	All Pastors	Multisite Beginners	Multisite Strategists	Planting Beginners	Planting Strategists	Location Partners
			Growth Strategy			

QII: What is the approximate number of adult attendees across all campuses and services affiliated with your church?

	All Pastors	Multisite Beginners	Multisite Strategists	Planting Beginners	Planting Strategists	Location Partners
Median	365 to 370	310 to 400	550	250 to 275	600 to 650	175

	All Pastors	Multisite Beginners	Multisite Strategists	Planting Beginners	Planting Strategists	Location Partners
			Growth Strategy			

Q12: As best you can, estimate the proportion of your congregation that falls into each of the following age categories. (Among pastors of one campus or church.) * Mean percentage

	All Pastors	Multisite Beginners	Multisite Strategists	Planting Beginners	Planting Strategists	Location Partners
Under 18	17%	19%	14%	19%	18%	15%
18 to 24	9%	12%	8%	10%	11%	7%
25 to 34	14%	14%	14%	16%	16%	11%
35 to 44	18%	17%	16%	21%	19%	16%
45 to 54	15%	16%	15%	14%	14%	16%
55 to 64	14%	10%	14%	14%	13%	15%
65 and older	19%	20%	24%	11%	15%	23%

	% All pastors	% Multisite beginners	Growth strategy % Multisite strategists	% Planting beginners	% Planting strategists	% Location partners

Q13: In what type of area is your church located?
(Among pastors of one campus or church.)

	% All pastors	% Multisite beginners	% Multisite strategists	% Planting beginners	% Planting strategists	% Location partners
Rural	9		17	6	9	6
Small town	35	13	24	45	22	52
Suburb	39	88	34	32	35	39
Urban	17		24	16	35	3

	All Pastors	Multisite Beginners	Growth Strategy			
			Multisite Strategists	Planting Beginners	Planting Strategists	Location Partners

Q14: How far is your church / campus from the sending church?
(% among those who are *not* at the sending church.)

	All Pastors	Multisite Beginners	Multisite Strategists	Planting Beginners	Planting Strategists	Location Partners
Median (in miles)	15	8 to 10	17	12	25	5 to 6

B. Methodology

The data contained in this report originated through a research study conducted by Barna Group of Ventura, California. The study was commissioned by Cornerstone Knowledge Network on behalf of Aspen Group and Fishhook.

Qualitative research for this study consisted of 31 individual interviews with church leaders of multisite and planting churches, including some consultants who have worked with numerous such churches over the years. These in-depth interviews were conducted either in-person at the 2015 Exponential West conference or via phone during October and November 2015.

The subsequent quantitative survey was administered online, March 7 to April 6, 2016, to leaders of churches that self-identify as one of the following:

- A multisite church (one church with two or more geographical locations) → *classified as multisite*
- A "reproducing" church (duplicated campuses and / or church plants) → *classified as a church plant*
- A "multiplying" church (multiple campuses that have birthed campuses and / or church plants that have planted churches) → *classified as a church plant*
- A multisite church network (multiple campuses and affiliated churches) → *classified as multisite*
- A central organization responsible for supporting or managing a group of related churches → *classified as a church plant*
- An individual congregation that is part of a larger church → *classified as a location partner*

In order to achieve a representative sample of multisite and planting churches, participants were invited from national lists of senior pastors and screened for inclusion based on their role (they answered "always" or "usually" when asked, "Are you involved in decisions about your church's growth—whether strategic or operational?").

After removing data from any churches that didn't have an *active* multisite or church planting ministry, our respondent set included 222 church leaders, 56 percent of whom are responsible for one location, and 44 percent of whom are responsible for multiple churches or campuses. The sampling error for the quantitative study is plus or minus 6.6 percent with a 95-percent confidence interval. Any differences called out between the comparison groups (five models of churches) are significantly different at the 95-percent confidence level, such that even these small sample sizes point to actual trends or unique perspectives among the different church types.

The most prevalent denominations that participated in this research are listed below. Of these, Southern Baptist and non-denominational churches are the most active church planters, while Methodists and Missouri Synod Lutherans are well represented among multisite churches and location partners. Other denominations are relatively evenly spread among the various models.

What is the denomination of your church?
(those over 3% only)

	ALL LEADERS
Baptist – Southern	22%
Methodist – United	16%
Baptist (all others)	8%
Lutheran – Missouri Synod (LCMS)	8%
Non-denominational / community / independent	8%
Assemblies of God	4%
Lutheran — Evangelical (ELCA)	3%

C.
Acknowledgements

Barna Group offers our sincere thanks to the Cornerstone Knowledge Network team, which includes talented folks from Aspen Group and Fishhook:

- Ed Bahler, CEO, Aspen Group

- Brad Eisenmann, President, Aspen Group

- Marian V. Liautaud, Director of Marketing, Aspen Group

- Evan McBroom, Founder and Creative Director, Fishhook

Barna also wishes to thank the contributors to *More Than Multisite*, Dave Travis and Bob Sawyer. Your experiences and insights help put these statistics into a human frame, reminding us that real people and faith communities are represented by the numbers.

The research team for this study is Brooke Hempell, Inga Dahlstedt and Pam Jacob. David Kinnaman contributed analysis and project leadership. Under the editorial direction of Roxanne Stone, Brooke Hempell, Alyce Youngblood and Aly Hawkins wrote *More Than Multisite*. Under the creative direction of Chaz Russo, Annette Allen designed the report and data visualizations. Brenda Usery managed production.

The *More Than Multisite* team also thanks our Barna colleagues Amy Brands, Chrisandra Bolton, Matt Carobini, Joyce Chiu, Bill Denzel, Traci Hochmuth, Jill Kinnaman, Elaine Klautzsch, Cory Maxwell-Coghlan, Josh Pearce, Megan Pritchett, Todd Sorenson and Todd White.

D. About the Research Partners

BARNA GROUP is a research firm dedicated to providing actionable insights on faith and culture, with a particular focus on the Christian church. In its 30-year history, Barna Group has conducted more than one million interviews in the course of hundreds of studies, and has become a go-to source for organizations that want to better understand a complex and changing world from a faith perspective. Barna's clients include a broad range of academic institutions, churches, non-profits and businesses, such as Alpha, the Templeton Foundation, Pepperdine University, Fuller Seminary, the Bill and Melinda Gates Foundation, the Maclellan Foundation, DreamWorks Animation, Focus Features, Habitat for Humanity, the Navigators, NBC-Universal, the ONE Campaign, Paramount Pictures, the Salvation Army, Walden Media, Sony and World Vision. The firm's studies are frequently quoted by major media outlets such as *The Economist*, BBC, CNN, *USA Today, the Wall Street Journal*, Fox News, Huffington Post, *The New York Times* and *the Los Angeles Times*.

barna.com

CORNERSTONE KNOWLEDGE NETWORK (CKN) exists to develop and disseminate meaningful knowledge that radically improves how facilities shape ministry. Co-founded by Aspen Group and other church industry specialists, CKN partners with some of today's most trusted research partners to help understand the intersection of culture, ministry, leadership and facilities.

theckn.com

ASPEN GROUP is a church design / build / furnish firm whose mission is to create space for ministry impact. Since 2004, Aspen Group has been the primary sponsor of research commissioned by CKN, including the CKN / Barna reports *More Than Multisite* and *Making Space for Millennials*. Aspen Group invests in research to help churches engage in the right conversations and enhance ministry effectiveness.

aspengroup.com

FISHHOOK is an innovative communications and creative services company that partners with churches, ministries and faith-based nonprofits, helping them communicate clearly, creatively and consistently. With proven approaches in all phases of ministry communications, Fishhook provides a wide variety of creative and strategic consultation. Fishhook's uniquely qualified team includes strategic thinkers, creative directors, project managers, graphic designers, writers, web developers and video storytellers.

fishhook.us

Design with Millennials in Mind

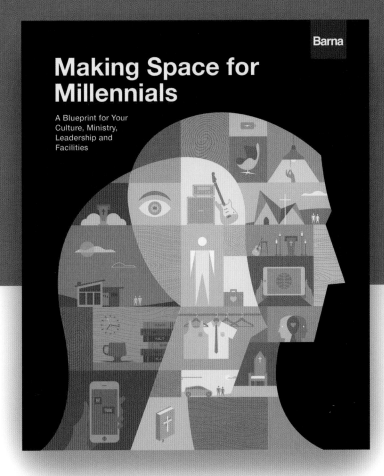

Barna

Making Space for Millennials

A Blueprint for Your Culture, Ministry, Leadership and Facilities

Use this book to

- Discover how churches are impacted by the values, allegiances, and assumptions of Millennials

- Hear Millennials' perspectives on worship and community spaces

- Learn from practitioners in culture, ministry, leadership, and facilities

- Gain valuable insights about how this generation views and relates to form and function

Faith communities and Christian organizations are struggling with how to make space for Millennials—not just appealing space in their buildings and gathering places, but also space in their institutional culture, ministry models, and leadership approach. This groundbreaking report, produced in partnership with Cornerstone Knowledge Network, is a handbook for turning information about Millennials into connections with Millennials in your church, school, or organization.

Whether you're a pastor, educator, youth or young adult ministry leader, nonprofit or business leader, or a parent, *Making Space for Millennials* is designed to help you make the most of your current and future partnerships with Millennials.

Purchase at
**barna.com
/makingspace**